THE HEART LUNGS AND BLOOD

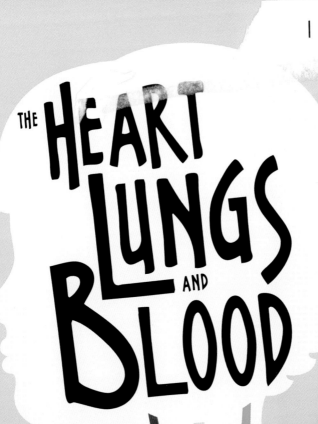

THE BRIGHT & BOLD HUMAN BODY

IZZI HOWELL

First published in Great Britain in 2019 by Wayland

Copyright © Hodder & Stoughton Limited, 2019

 Produced for Wayland by
White-Thomson Publishing Ltd
www.wtpub.co.uk

Editor: Izzi Howell
Designer: Dan Prescott, Couper Street Type Co.
Illustrations: Techtype (pp 10–11 and 14–15)

HB ISBN: 978 1 5263 1041 5
PB ISBN: 978 1 5263 1042 2
10 9 8 7 6 5 4 3 2 1

MIX
Paper from
responsible sources
FSC® C104740
FSC
www.fsc.org

Wayland
An imprint of Hachette Children's Group
Part of Hodder & Stoughton
Carmelite House
50 Victoria Embankment
London EC4Y 0DZ

An Hachette UK Company
www.hachette.co.uk
www.hachettechildrens.co.uk

Printed in China

Picture acknowledgements
Alamy: Science Photo Library 13, Science Picture Co 19; Getty: Nerthuz 9b, BahadirTanriover
10l, Maartje van Caspel 15t, arkira 17t, MadPierre 17b, Ogphoto 20t, PeterHermesFurian 23t,
normaals 23b, Ed Reschke 25r, SUSUMU NISHINAGA 29b; Shutterstock: Hi-Vector cover,
Tomacco 4r, Macrovector 4–5c, Richman Photo 5r, Luciano Cosmo 6, Jose Luis Calvo 7,
cash1994 8, NotionPic 9t, VectorMine 12 and 28, gritsalak karalak 13t and 23c, Designua 16
and 25l, udaix 18–19, elenabsl 20b and 21, ShadeDesign 22, corbac40 24–25c, TippaPatt 27,
ellepigrafica 29t.

All design elements from Shutterstock.

Contents

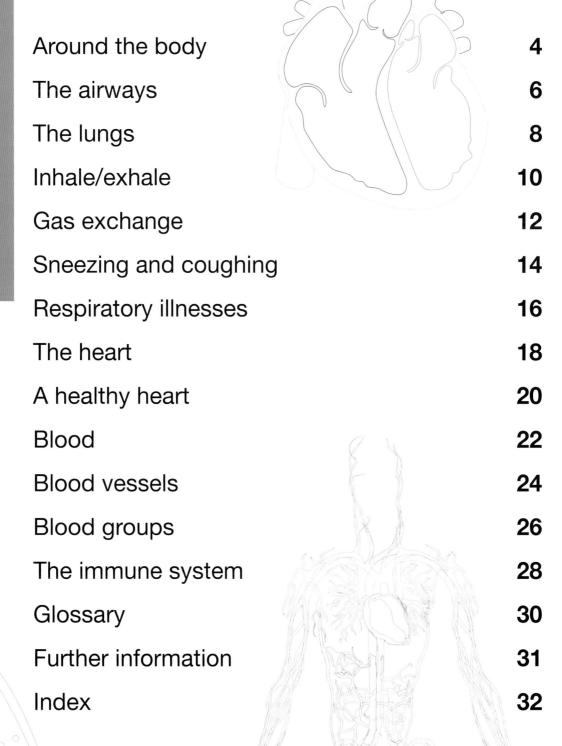

Around the body

Our bodies are made up of trillions of cells. Every cell needs oxygen to produce energy. We need energy for everything that we do, so delivering oxygen to our cells is a vital process.

The respiratory system transports oxygen into the body for cells to use. The process in which cells use oxygen to produce energy is called aerobic respiration. Aerobic respiration also produces carbon dioxide. This is a waste gas that we don't need in our bodies.

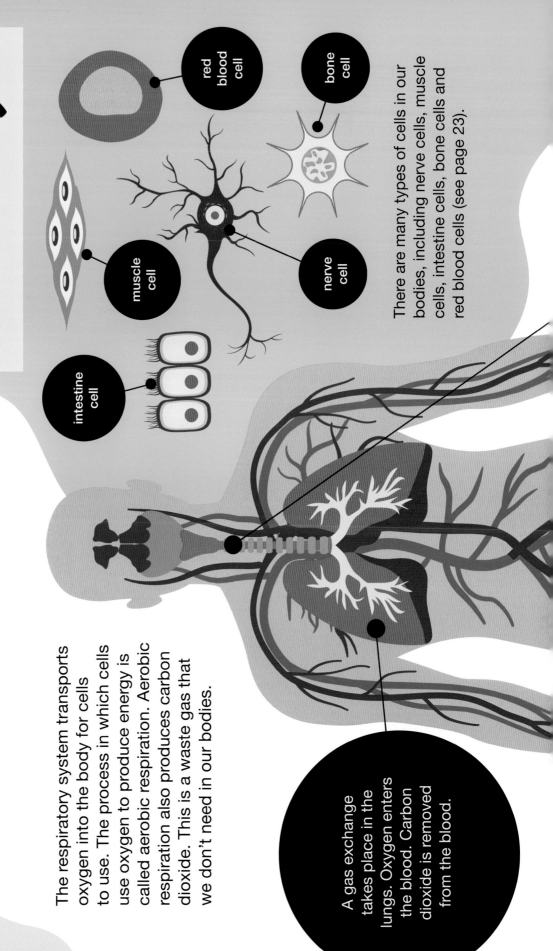

red blood cell

bone cell

muscle cell

nerve cell

intestine cell

There are many types of cells in our bodies, including nerve cells, muscle cells, intestine cells, bone cells and red blood cells (see page 23).

A gas exchange takes place in the lungs. Oxygen enters the blood. Carbon dioxide is removed from the blood.

Carbon dioxide leaves the body through the airways.

A network of arteries (shown in white) carries blood to the brain and across the head.

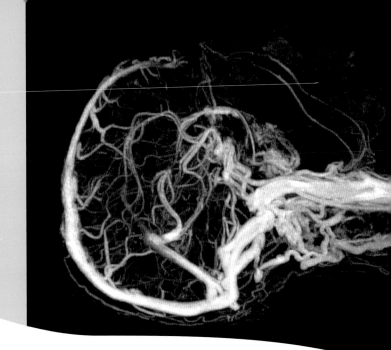

37.2 trillion

the number of cells in the human body, all of which need to be supplied with oxygen

Oxygen and carbon dioxide travel around the body through the cardiovascular system. They are carried in the blood through a network of arteries, veins and capillaries. The heart acts as a pump, moving this blood around the body to and from cells.

The airways

When we breathe in, air travels through the airways to the lungs. The airways include the nose, mouth, throat and trachea.

Most air enters the body through the nostrils. Mucus and tiny hairs filter the air as it travels through the nose. They trap dust and germs that could damage the lungs.

Some air enters through the mouth.

18,000– 20,000 litres

the amount of air that passes through an adult's nose every day – that's a lorry-load of air

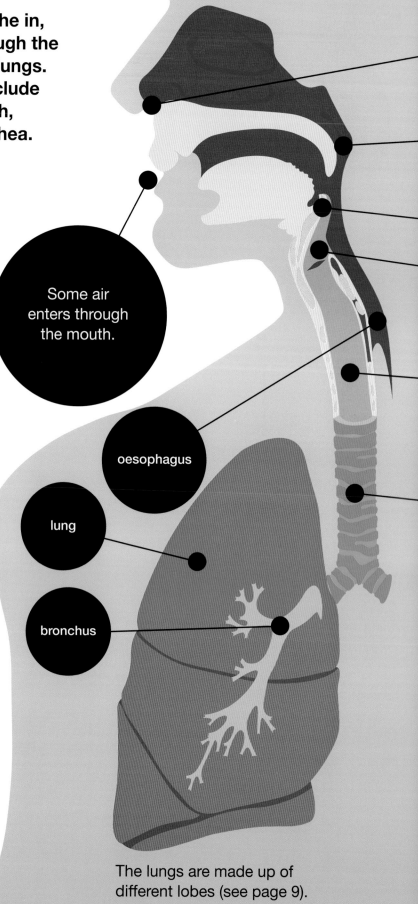

oesophagus

lung

bronchus

The lungs are made up of different lobes (see page 9).

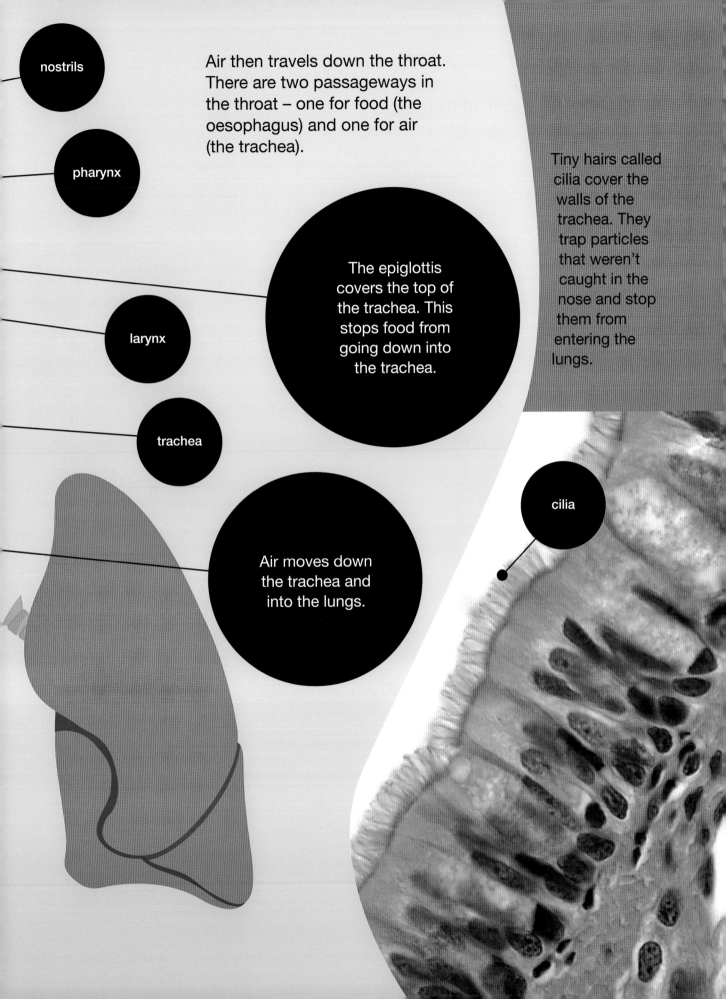

nostrils

pharynx

Air then travels down the throat. There are two passageways in the throat – one for food (the oesophagus) and one for air (the trachea).

Tiny hairs called cilia cover the walls of the trachea. They trap particles that weren't caught in the nose and stop them from entering the lungs.

larynx

The epiglottis covers the top of the trachea. This stops food from going down into the trachea.

trachea

cilia

Air moves down the trachea and into the lungs.

The lungs are at the end of the airways and respiratory system. In the lungs, oxygen (O_2) from the air enters the blood and carbon dioxide (CO_2) is removed from the blood. This is known as gas exchange (see pages 12–13).

The bronchi are the two airways that come from the trachea into the lungs.

Bronchioles are smaller airways that come off the bronchi.

The bronchioles connect the bronchi to the alveoli. Air travels through the 1 mm-wide passageways to the alveoli, where oxygen enters the blood and carbon dioxide is removed.

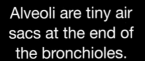

Alveoli are tiny air sacs at the end of the bronchioles.

The left lung is smaller than the right lung because it shares its space with the heart, which is tilted slightly to the left. The left lung is made up of two lobes, while the right lung has three lobes.

lobes

1

2

3

1

2

2,414 km

the length of the airways in the lungs

Healthy lungs (left) are pink. The lungs of a smoker (right) are unhealthy and dark from particles in the cigarettes that block the bronchioles.

When we inhale (breathe in) and exhale (breathe out), our ribs, lungs and diaphragm change position and shape. This movement pulls air into the body and pushes it out again.

air in

diaphragm

The diaphragm is a large, dome-shaped band of muscle between the lungs and the stomach.

The diaphragm contracts and moves down to let more air in.

inhale

During inhalation, the muscles in the ribcage and the diaphragm tighten. This makes the ribcage expand upwards and outwards to make more space. The increase in chest size creates an area of low pressure inside the body. Air is sucked into the area of low pressure, travelling through the airways and into the lungs.

As the diaphragm relaxes nd the ribcage returns to its original size and position, there is less space available in the chest. As a result, air is pushed out of the body through the airways.

The lungs expand as they fill with air. They get smaller as air leaves the body.

air out

3–5 cm

the average increase in the circumference of an adult's ribcage during inhalation

exhale

Gas exchange

Gas exchange takes place in the alveoli (see pages 8–9). Here oxygen (O_2), from the air passes into the bloodstream and carbon dioxide (CO_2) is removed.

There are around 700 million alveoli in an adult's lungs. Although they are very small, there are so many that if they were all spread out flat on the ground, they would cover a tennis court. They are surrounded by tiny blood vessels, called capillaries (see page 25). The walls of the alveoli and the capillaries are so thin that gases can pass through them.

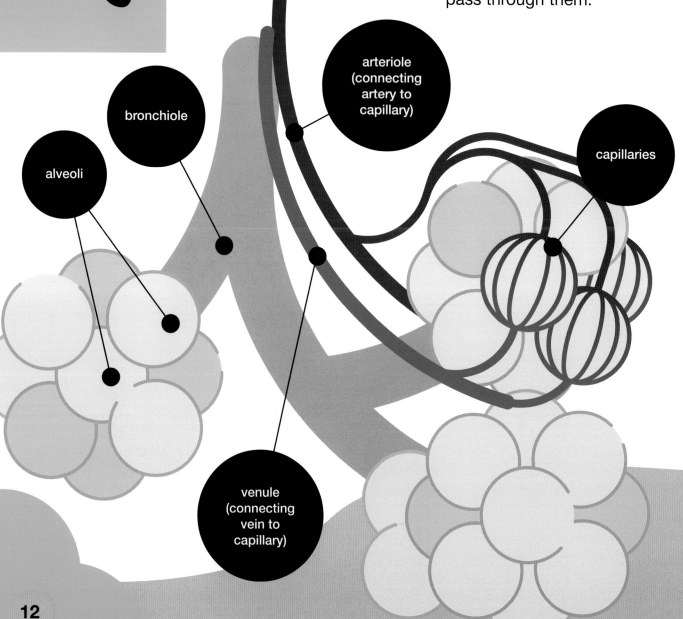

arteriole (connecting artery to capillary)

bronchiole

capillaries

alveoli

venule (connecting vein to capillary)

0.2 mm

the average diameter of an alveolus (singular of alveoli) – about the same width as a human hair

CO₂

$$CO_2$$

O₂

$$O_2$$

carbon dioxide out

oxygen in

During inhalation, the alveoli fill with oxygen-rich air. Some of this oxygen passes through the walls of the alveoli into the capillary, where it is picked up by red blood cells.

Red blood cells also carry carbon dioxide, a waste gas from aerobic respiration (see pages 4–5), from cells to the lungs. This passes from the capillary into the alveoli. It leaves the body when we exhale.

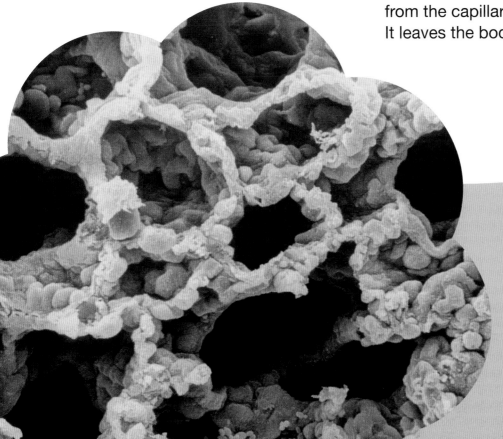

This microscopic image shows the air sacs of the alveoli and the walls where gas exchange takes place.

Sneezing and coughing

It is important for the airways to stay clear so that the body can receive oxygen. Sneezing and coughing remove particles from our airways so that we can breathe properly.

40,000
the number of saliva and mucus droplets that are released by one sneeze

Nerve endings send a signal to the brain, which triggers the sneeze or cough reflex. First, the body takes a deep breath in.

A sneeze or a cough happens when nerve endings in the nose or airways sense dust or dirt particles, pollen, or mucus.

Sneezing and coughing also get rid of mucus that develops during an illness. This mucus often contains bacteria or viruses from the illness. These pathogens are sprayed out during a cough or sneeze. They can be passed on to other people, spreading the illness.

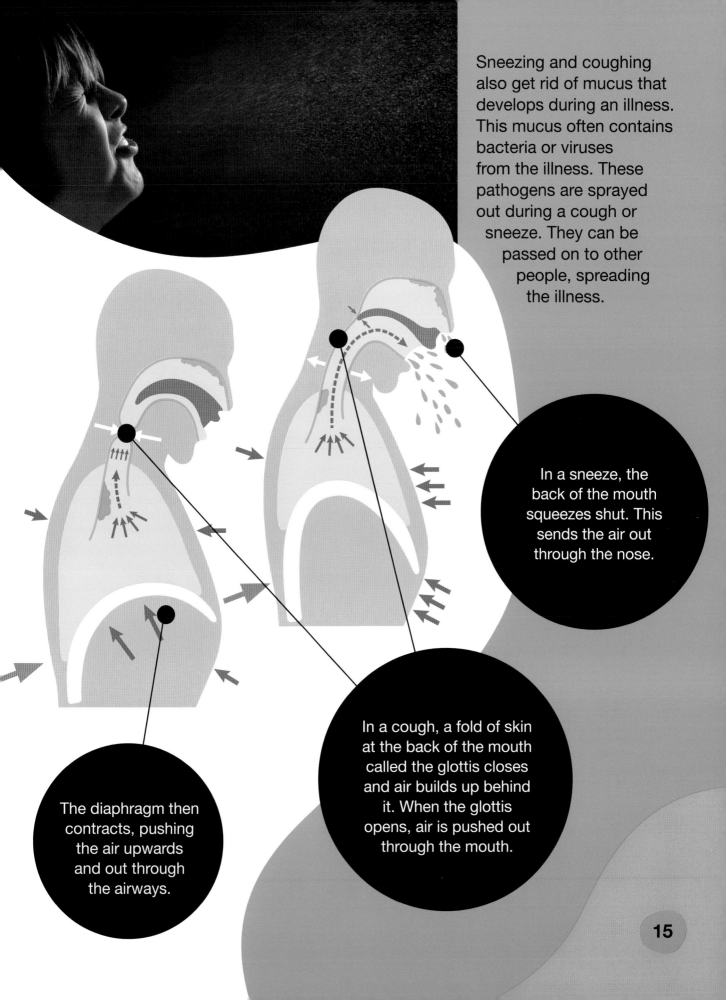

In a sneeze, the back of the mouth squeezes shut. This sends the air out through the nose.

In a cough, a fold of skin at the back of the mouth called the glottis closes and air builds up behind it. When the glottis opens, air is pushed out through the mouth.

The diaphragm then contracts, pushing the air upwards and out through the airways.

Respiratory illnesses

The respiratory system is often affected by illnesses. These range from mild diseases, such as the common cold, to serious conditions, such as asthma and pneumonia.

Infections are common in the respiratory system. Bacteria and viruses are breathed in through the nose and mouth and can affect areas along the airways. The most common respiratory disease is the cold, which affects the nose and the throat. Pneumonia is a serious infection of the lungs.

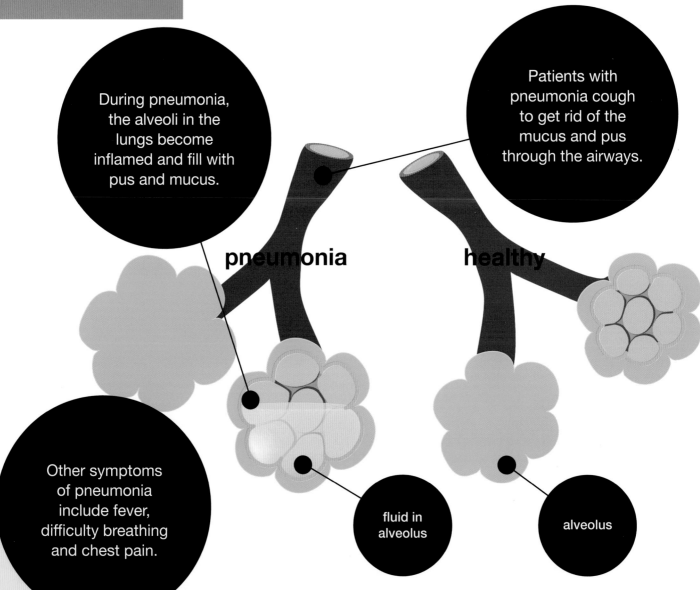

During pneumonia, the alveoli in the lungs become inflamed and fill with pus and mucus.

Patients with pneumonia cough to get rid of the mucus and pus through the airways.

pneumonia

healthy

Other symptoms of pneumonia include fever, difficulty breathing and chest pain.

fluid in alveolus

alveolus

Asthma is an inflammation of the airways and lungs. The airways become smaller, which makes it harder to breathe. During an asthma attack, the airways can close almost entirely. Some people are born with asthma, while some people develop it because of air pollution or an allergy to pollen.

Some people with asthma have more mucus than normal. They cough to get rid of it.

The airways of people with asthma are always narrow, but they become even narrower during an asthma attack.

normal

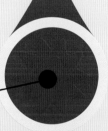
asthma

asthma attack

7–10%
the percentage of children that have asthma

Inhalers filled with medicine help to lessen the symptoms of asthma by reducing inflammation and widening the airways.

The heart is a powerful muscle that pumps oxygenated blood around the body, on its way to cells. It is positioned between the lungs, tilted slightly to the left of the body.

The heart is divided into left and right sides. Each side has two chambers. The top chambers are called atria and the bottom chambers are called ventricles.

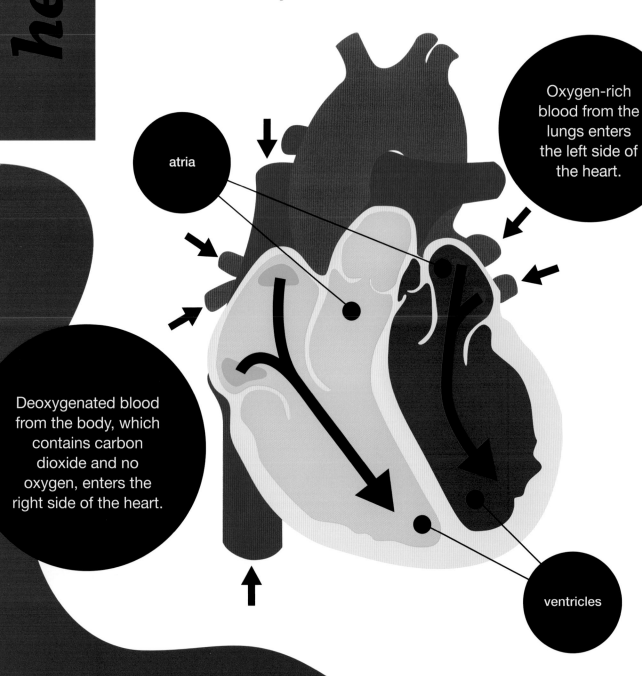

atria

Oxygen-rich blood from the lungs enters the left side of the heart.

Deoxygenated blood from the body, which contains carbon dioxide and no oxygen, enters the right side of the heart.

ventricles

The oxygen-rich blood goes from the heart to the rest of the body.

7,500 litres
the quantity of blood pumped by an adult heart every day – the equivalent of over 20 bathtubs

The deoxygenated blood is pumped back to the lungs, so that it can become oxygenated through gas exchange.

Natural electrical impulses make the heart muscles contract and relax. First, the atria contract, pushing blood into the ventricles. Then, the ventricles contract, pushing blood out of the heart.

This is a pulmonary valve – one of four valves in the heart. Valves open to let blood flow through and then close to stop it from flowing backwards. The sound of a heartbeat is actually the sound of a valve closing.

A healthy heart

It is important to keep the heart healthy and working well. Doing exercise and eating a balanced diet help to prevent problems such as heart disease and heart attacks.

This is the artery of someone suffering from heart disease. The purple area is the fatty material blocking the artery.

Heart disease is a build up of fatty material in the coronary arteries – the arteries that supply blood to the heart. The arteries become narrow, which makes it hard for the heart to receive enough oxygen-rich blood. This is painful, uncomfortable and dangerous.

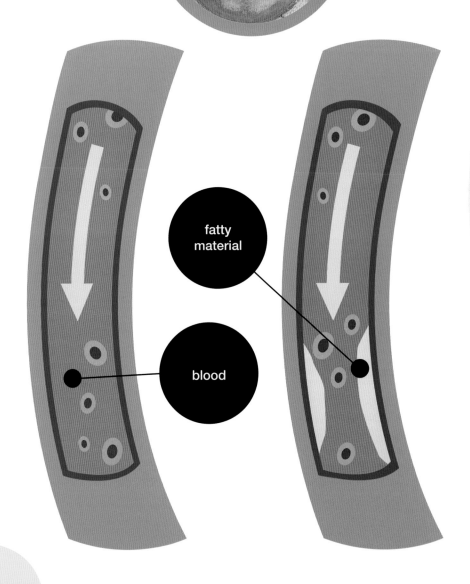

fatty material

blood

If a piece of the fatty material breaks off, it can form a blood clot. A blood clot can block a coronary artery, stopping oxygen from reaching the heart. Without oxygen, the heart muscles begin to die. This is known as a heart attack. Heart attacks can be fatal.

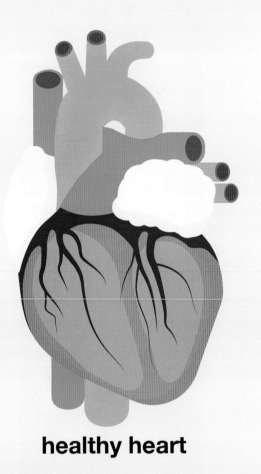

healthy heart

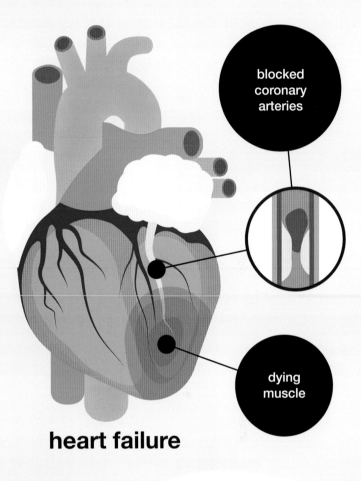

blocked coronary arteries

dying muscle

heart failure

24%

the increased risk of developing heart disease of a smoker compared to a non-smoker

Eating a healthy, balanced diet and doing regular exercise are the best ways to keep the heart healthy. Eating too much salt, smoking and obesity increase the risk of developing heart disease. Most people affected by heart disease and heart attacks are adults, but it is important for young people to develop good health habits.

Blood

Blood is made up of red blood cells, white blood cells, platelets and plasma. It transports materials around the body, and it is also involved in the body's immune system (see pages 28–29).

5 litres

the amount of blood in the average adult's body, around 7% of the total body weight

Plasma is one of the main ingredients in blood. It is a liquid, mainly made up of water. Plasma carries nutrients, hormones and waste around the body. Red blood cells are the other main component. As we've seen, they transport oxygen to cells around the body. Platelets help blood to clot, while white blood cells are part of the immune system.

blood structure

54% plasma

<1% white blood cells

<1% platelets

45% red blood cells

platelets

red blood cells

plasma

white blood cells

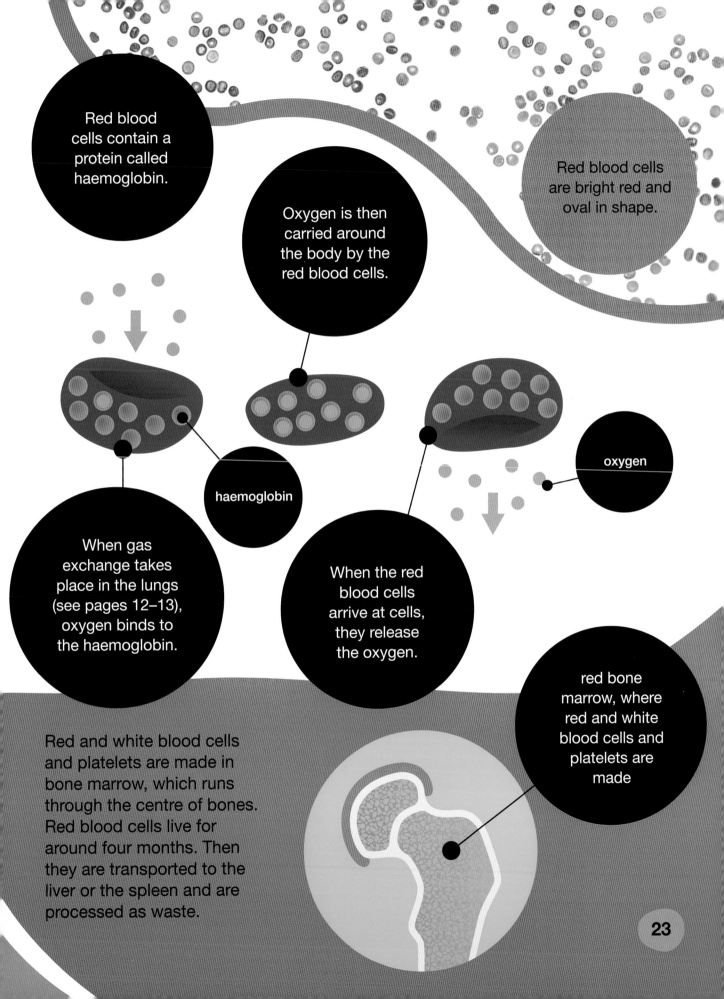

Red blood cells contain a protein called haemoglobin.

Red blood cells are bright red and oval in shape.

Oxygen is then carried around the body by the red blood cells.

haemoglobin

oxygen

When gas exchange takes place in the lungs (see pages 12–13), oxygen binds to the haemoglobin.

When the red blood cells arrive at cells, they release the oxygen.

red bone marrow, where red and white blood cells and platelets are made

Red and white blood cells and platelets are made in bone marrow, which runs through the centre of bones. Red blood cells live for around four months. Then they are transported to the liver or the spleen and are processed as waste.

Blood vessels

Blood vessels carry blood to and from the heart and around the body. There are three different types of blood vessels – arteries, veins and capillaries.

100,000 km

the combined length of blood vessels in the human body – enough to go around the world two and a half times

The vena cava is the body's largest vein. It leads back to the heart and returns blood from the entire body.

arteries (red)

veins (blue)

The aorta is the largest artery in the body. It comes directly out of the heart.

Capillaries are the tiny blood vessels that go to individual cells and tissue. They split apart and join back together, forming a web. The walls of capillaries are so thin that oxygen, nutrients and water can pass through the wall and into the cell. Carbon dioxide passes the other way and enters the bloodstream in the capillary.

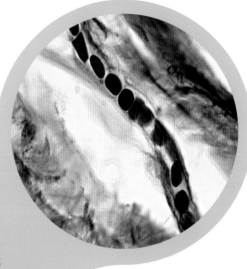

Most capillaries are so narrow that red blood cells can only pass through in single file.

Arteries carry oxygen-rich blood from the heart to cells around the body. The blood inside arteries is at high pressure, so arteries have thick walls to withstand this. Veins carry blood back to the heart. The blood in veins is at a lower pressure, so they have thinner walls.

vein

There are valves in veins to stop blood flowing in the wrong direction. Every time the heart beats, valves open to let blood through. The valves then close to stop the blood flowing backwards.

artery

Arteries do not need valves because the pressure from the heart is so strong that blood is only able to flow in one direction.

Blood groups

There are four different types of blood – A, B, AB and O. Each type of blood can also be positive (+) or negative (-), for example B+ or O-. Each blood group has very slightly different red blood cells and antibodies.

Blood groups are very important when it comes to blood transfusions. If someone loses a lot of blood in an accident or through illness, they might need an injection of blood taken from another person's body.

Blood transfusions have to be from the correct blood group (see chart to the right). Some groups of blood can be given to people from other groups and some can't. It can make people very sick if they receive the wrong type of blood.

Blood from positive groups can only be given to people with positive blood. Blood from negative groups can be given to anyone.

blood-type compatibility chart

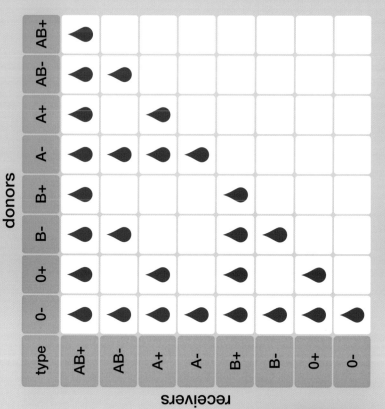

donors

type	0-	0+	B-	B+	A-	A+	AB-	AB+
AB+	●	●	●	●	●	●	●	●
AB-	●		●		●		●	
A+	●	●			●	●		
A-	●				●			
B+	●	●	●	●				
B-	●		●					
0+	●	●						
0-	●							

receivers

Blood groups are passed down from parents to children. Each person has two blood group genes. One comes from each parent.

A and B blood group genes are dominant. This means if someone has one of these genes, this will be their blood group.

A and B blood group genes can combine. If someone has one of each, their blood group is AB.

39%

the proportion of the worldwide population with O+ group blood

If both parents have a negative blood group, their child will also be negative. Otherwise, their child could be positive or negative.

Blood is tested in hospitals so that the blood group can be identified.

blood type B

blood type A

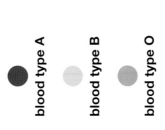

| blood type A | blood type AB | blood type B | blood type O |

● **blood type A**

● **blood type B**

● **blood type O**

O blood group genes are recessive. This means a person will only have this blood group if both of their blood group genes are O.

The immune system

The body's immune system protects it from pathogens, such as bacteria, that can cause disease. Blood plays an important role in the immune system, helping to close wounds and fighting dangerous pathogens.

When we cut ourselves, platelets in the blood clump together at the wound. They plug the hole to stop blood from leaving the body and to stop pathogens from entering the body.

Platelets and red blood cells gather around the wound.

Platelets release a chemical that makes plasma turn into a stringy substance called fibrin.

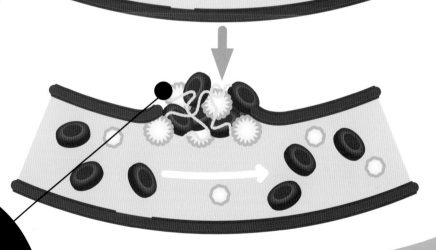

The fibrin forms a mesh across the wound, which traps the platelets and blood cells. This dries into a scab, closing the wound.

Red blood cells and platelets (pink) trapped in a fibrin net can be seen through a microscope.

When pathogens get inside the body, different types of white blood cells help to destroy them. Some white blood cells surround and ingest pathogens. Others produce antibodies that stick on to pathogens and stop them from damaging the body.

150,000–400,000 per cubic mm

the average number of platelets in blood

A white blood cell surrounds a pathogen.

The broken-down pieces of the pathogen are ejected from the white blood cell.

pathogens

antibodies

It ingests the pathogen.

The white blood cell breaks down the pathogen into small, harmless pieces.

Glossary

aerobic respiration – the process in which cells use oxygen to produce energy from food

alveoli – very small air sacs in the lungs where gas exchange takes place

antibody – something that sticks to pathogens and destroys them

artery – a blood vessel that carries blood from the heart to other parts of the body

capillary – a very thin blood vessel

carbon dioxide – a waste gas produced by cells during aerobic respiration

cardiovascular system – the system of the heart and blood vessels

cell – the smallest living part of a living thing

clot – to turn from a liquid into a solid lump

diaphragm – the large band of muscle between the lungs and the stomach

gene – a part of a living thing's DNA that is passed on from its parents and which controls different qualities, such as hair colour or blood group

haemoglobin – a substance in red blood cells that binds to oxygen and carries it around the body

hormone – a chemical that controls important processes in the body

immune system – the cells and systems in the body that protect it from disease

nutrient – a substance that a living thing needs to grow and be healthy

oxygen – a gas found in the air that cells need to produce energy

pathogen – a very small organism that can cause disease, such as a virus or bacteria

plasma – a liquid that forms 54 per cent of human blood

platelets – cells in the blood that clot at a wound to stop blood from escaping

respiratory system – the system of the airways and lungs

trachea – the tube that carries air from the top of the throat to the lungs

vein – a blood vessel that carries blood to the heart from other parts of the body

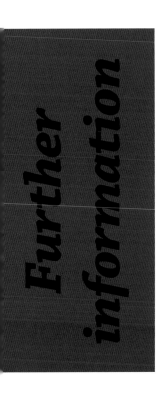
Further reading

In the Human Body (Cause, Effect and Chaos) by Paul Mason (Wayland, 2018)

Human Body (Infomojis) by John Richards and Ed Simkins (Wayland, 2018)

Your Breathtaking Lungs and Rocking Respiratory System by Paul Mason (Wayland, 2016)

Websites

kidshealth.org/en/kids/rsquiz.html

Take a quiz about the respiratory system.

www.bbc.com/bitesize/articles/zs8f8mn

Watch a video about the circulatory system.

www.scienceforkidsclub.com/heart.html

Learn more about the heart.

Index